victory

A SEVEN-STEP STRATEGY
FOR RESISTING TEMPTATION
AND OVERCOMING SIN

Jim Schettler

First published in 2019 by Striving Together Publications, a ministry of Lancaster Baptist Church, Lancaster, CA 93535. Striving Together Publications is committed to providing tried, trusted, and proven books that will further equip local churches to carry out the Great Commission. Your comments and suggestions are valued.

Striving Together Publications
4020 E. Lancaster Blvd.
Lancaster, CA 93535
800.201.7748

Cover design by Levi Jones
Writing assistance by Anna Gregory

The author and publication team have given every effort to give proper credit to quotes and thoughts that are not original with the author. It is not our intent to claim originality with any quote or thought that could not readily be tied to an original source.

ISBN 978-1-59894-393-1

Printed in the United States of America

DEDICATION

The Lord in His mercy and grace has allowed me to have victory in and through Christ and because of that, I want to please Him all of my life. Besides that transforming truth, my Lord has given me a virtuous wife Marilee and three godly, passionate sons, Ben, Luke, and Drew, who motivate me to continue in victory. It is for my family I dedicate this book.

CONTENTS

War Zone

Everyone's morning looks different.

Perhaps you are a mom of young children. Before the first, "Mooooommm, I need you!" begins, you try to carve out a few minutes to read your Bible and drink a cup of coffee in blissful silence. But when the kids wake up, you're swept up in the rush of packing lunches, preparing breakfast, and getting little people out the door in time for school.

Or maybe you're a college student. Usually, your alarm goes off while it's still dark outside. As you get ready for the day, you review your class notes for the quiz you have in history. Finally, with four minutes before class starts, you grab your backpack and a granola bar for breakfast and race across campus.

Perhaps you're retired. Your mornings are a little more laid back as you sit on the front porch, read the newspaper, and enjoy breakfast with your spouse.

Maybe you're in the middle of your career. Before 9:30 hits, you've commuted in rush hour traffic, answered emails, taken phone calls, and attended a meeting. As you pause to catch your breath and glance at your planner, you know your hectic day is just beginning.

You might be in full-time Christian ministry. Some mornings are structured and predictable. Others, however, are the opposite because of an unexpected phone call or ministry need.

I don't know if your morning is similar to one just described or completely different. But I can guarantee one similarity between your morning and every other Christian's morning. No matter what stage of life you're in, how long you've been saved, or how mature you are in your Christian walk, the second you open your eyes, you enter a war zone.

As believers, we have an enemy actively on the prowl to tempt us to sin and destroy our lives. Our own flesh is pulling us toward sinful desires, fighting against the new creature God has made us in Christ (2 Corinthians 5:17). Yes, from within and without, we are in the middle of a battle against sin.

How many times have we gotten up in the morning with a hymn on our lips, determined to live for the Lord? Maybe God gave us a special verse in our devotions—one we're committed to implementing in our lives. We've prayed and asked the Lord to fill us with His Spirit. We're ready to face the day...or so we think.

But before lunchtime even hits, we've conceded defeat in our spiritual battle. We snapped at the kids, yelled at the guy who cut us off on the freeway, gossiped about a coworker, said something unkind about a friend—you fill in the blank. Shaking our heads, we say, "What's the use? I can't get victory in the Christian life. It's too hard."

Maybe there's one sin in particular that you're trying to defeat. It could be anger you can't seem to control. It might be lust you've struggled with since you were a teenager. It could be worry or doubt that plagues your mind. It seems no matter how hard you try, no matter how much gritted-teeth effort you put into it, you just can't get victory. Oh, you've read promises of victory in the Bible—in fact, you might even have a couple of verses taped on your bathroom mirror. But every time this specific temptation comes your way, you succumb. You've reached the point where you're discouraged, defeated, and ready to give up.

The devil wants us to think that living the victorious Christian life is impossible. He knows that if he can get us to admit defeat, he's hindered our effectiveness for God. He wants to trick us into believing we have to live under sin's power.

But I'm tired of Christians buying into this lie of defeat. Because Jesus conquered sin and death, we can say with the apostle Paul, "But thanks be to God, which giveth us the victory through our Lord Jesus Christ" (1 Corinthians 15:57). Victory in the Christian life isn't just a nice idea; it's something God wants us as His children to personally experience. The victory is already ours through Jesus, but it's up to us to claim it.

As Christians, we're commanded to have victory. First Thessalonians 4:3–4 commands, "For this is the will of God, even your sanctification, that ye should abstain from fornication: That every one of you should know how to possess his vessel in sanctification and honour." We don't have to wonder what God wants for our lives—He shows us in these verses. He wants us to possess our vessel (our lives and bodies) in sanctification and honour.

The word *sanctification* is key to understanding the rest of this book. The second we trusted Christ as our Saviour, we received salvation. What we sometimes don't realize, however, is that our salvation has three parts—past, present, and future. The word *salvation* is sometimes used interchangeably throughout Scripture for all three, and it's important that we know how to distinguish between them.

The first part of salvation is *justification,* meaning we were declared righteous. Romans 10:13 states, "For whosoever shall call upon the name of the Lord shall be saved." In this verse, *saved* means rescued from the penalty of sin.

The second part of salvation is *sanctification.* While justification occurs just once, sanctification is a consistently active process. I like to think of it as the moment I was saved, the Holy Spirit came into my heart with a scrub brush and a can of Ajax, helping me to clean up the dirty areas of sin in my heart and life. Philippians 2:12 expresses this concept, stating, "Wherefore, my beloved, as ye have always obeyed, not as in my presence only, but now much more in my absence, work out your own salvation with fear and trembling." Paul isn't telling the Philippians to work *for* their salvation. He's telling them to work *out* their salvation—to take the gift God gave them and put it into use by growing in the Lord. Now that we're saved, we have new life. Sin no longer has power over us—we have power over sin.

The final part of salvation is *glorification.* The Christian life is wonderful, but it's also difficult. No matter how long we've been saved, we will always struggle with sin. And that's one of the many reasons why I'm thankful for the hope of Heaven. When we die, our physical bodies will be glorified, and we'll be in the physical presence of Christ, saved from the presence of sin.

We might not have fully understood it at the time, but when we accepted Christ, we immediately received justification, and He began the sanctification process— what we're going to focus on in these pages. We're no longer under sin's penalty, but we still have Satan and our old, sinful flesh tempting us to do wrong. Now, living in victory isn't just a theoretical concept, it's something we can and are commanded to do.

God promises a blessing and a crown of life for enduring temptation. James 1:12–16 tells us, "Blessed is the man that endureth temptation: for when he is tried, he shall receive the crown of life, which the Lord hath promised to them that love him. Let no man say when he is tempted, I am tempted of God: for God cannot be tempted with evil, neither tempteth he any man: But every man is tempted, when he is drawn away of his own lust, and enticed. Then when lust hath conceived, it bringeth forth sin: and sin, when it is finished, bringeth forth death. Do not err, my beloved brethren."

Throughout my Christian life, I've heard many men say (and even believed it myself at one point) that being tempted is not wrong—yielding to sin is wrong. But based on the above verses, I believe that we can sin by tempting ourselves. We can be drawn away by our own lusts—by putting ourselves in a situation that causes us to sin. Yet the Bible commands us "…put ye on the Lord Jesus Christ, and make not provision for the flesh, to fulfil the lusts thereof" (Romans 13:14). It is much easier to avoid temptation than to resist temptation. And the sooner we learn to avoid temptation, the better we will become at resisting temptation.

The last part of our passage states, "Do not err, my beloved brethren." By this command, we see that not only is victory possible, it's commanded.

No matter if you're facing a persistent sin in your life, curious about what God says about living victoriously, or somewhere in between, this book is for you. When we were saved, God gave us everything we needed to live victoriously. It doesn't matter how long we've struggled with a specific sin, how many times we've tried to get victory, or what the sin is—we can get victory. That's a direct promise from God: "There hath no temptation taken you but such as is common to man: but God is faithful, who will not suffer you to be tempted above that ye are able; but will with the temptation also make a way to escape, that ye may be able to bear it" (1 Corinthians 10:13).

My prayer is that by the time you finish reading the last sentence in this book, you'll walk away, not just with the head knowledge of Christian living, but with practical, biblical steps to victory—a battle strategy.

Each of the following chapter titles begins with one of the seven letters of *victory*, forming an acrostic of the word. At the end of each chapter, I've provided suggestions of practical, spiritual exercises that will help you make the principle a part of your everyday life. I encourage you to practice the exercises for each truth.

Let's begin unpacking these principles together. We have some battles to win!

1

V - **Vigilantly** Guard against Sin

Have you ever known what a word meant but then experienced an event that added depth of meaning in your mind to the word? That happened to me with the word *vigilant*.

Years ago, I was preaching a few evenings in East Chicago, Indiana. A friend of mine in the congregation worked for the police force and invited me to go along on a ride one night in a patrol car.

Immediately, I said yes. (I don't think I had fully considered that East Chicago, Indiana, was, at that time, the murder capital of the United States.)

As the night of the ride along came, I was so excited that I think I preached about ten minutes. As soon as the service ended, I hurried to change into casual clothes.

When I went outside, I saw a police car with an officer leaning against it, and my friend introduced me to this officer who was going to take me along on the ride. After we introduced ourselves, he reached into the squad car and pulled out two items: a gun and a bulletproof vest.

Honestly, I didn't think he was serious at first. "You've got to be kidding me," I said, half-laughing. "I'm not wearing that. And I'm definitely not taking a gun."

The officer looked at me straight in the eyes. "You don't go with me without these two things." I have to admit that a little of the excitement wore off when I realized he was completely serious.

As I walked back to the church to put the vest on, I realized I was literally shaking. I thought to myself, "If my wife could see me now, she'd kill me!" Then, the thought comfortingly jumped into my mind, "But then, I might die anyway."

As I got into the back of the squad car, I was a mix of nerves and excitement. Fortunately, the night was fairly quiet, and I began to relax and enjoy the experience. That is, until we got our first call about an hour into our time.

The officer turned back to look at me and said, "This is going to be exciting—it's a domestic case."

With the car's sirens blaring, we raced to the scene. The second we pulled up, I could hear a husband and wife screaming at each other, and, to say the least, it sounded volatile. When the officer opened the door for me to step out, I noticed dozens, if not hundreds, of strange metal objects on the sidewalk. I bent down to pick one up, asking, "What is this?"

The officer responded, "Oh, those are AK-47 shell casings. You should have been here last week! It was quite the place."

Instantly, I dropped the casing on the ground and got back in the car. "Wait, wait!" The officer called after me. "Where are you going? We're going in, man!"

Reluctantly, I followed the officer into the house. If I could pick one word to describe my actions the rest of the night, that word would be *vigilant*.

Vigilant means "alertly watchful, especially to avoid danger." If you check your dictionary, you'll probably find a picture of me walking into that house next to the definition of vigilant.

As I thought back on my experience, I began to ask myself, "Am I that vigilant when it comes to sin? Am I that on guard to potential pitfalls in my life?" As Christians, we have a target on our backs. Satan doesn't just want us to fall, he wants us destroyed.

How can we expect to experience victory in our lives if we aren't even aware of the battle around us? The devil is not a cartoon drawing of a man in red with horns and a pitch fork; he's incredibly real and powerful. He watches for our weaknesses and capitalizes on them. He actively seeks to pull us into sin. In fact, just as much as we need to be aware of Satan's attacks, we need to be aware of our own weaknesses. Let's explore these two areas in which we need to practice vigilance.

Be Vigilant about the Devil

First Peter 5:8 draws a sobering parallel between Satan's attack and a lion seeking its prey: "Be sober, be vigilant; because your adversary the devil, as a roaring lion, walketh about, seeking whom he may devour."

Can't you almost hear Peter's voice in the back of your mind as you read this verse? "Christian, listen up! You've got an enemy in the devil. He's not to be fooled with—he is actively seeking to destroy you and ruin your life. Be vigilant! This is important!"

If you're saved, you're in the battle of your life. I think we can sometimes live our lives thinking that the devil is after someone else. Yet no one is immune to the devil's attacks. The devil isn't just looking to pick off your pastor or a Christian leader in your life. He is actively looking for an opportunity to destroy you, and he's willing to use every trick that he can to get you to fall. That's why Peter, under the inspiration of the Holy Spirit, used such strong words. The Lord wanted you and me to grasp the gravity of the spiritual battle being waged for our hearts.

We will never experience true victory in our Christian lives until we wake up and determine that we're going to be on guard. The instant we show weakness, Satan takes advantage. In fact, we're commanded in the Bible, "Wherefore let him that thinketh he standeth take heed lest he fall" (1 Corinthians 10:12). Too many people have deceived themselves into believing that they are strong enough to resist temptation—with tragic consequences.

You see, no one ever wakes up and thinks, "You know what? Today sounds like a great day to commit adultery and lose my marriage." Or, "I'm going to become an alcoholic. Maybe I'll lose everything and everyone dear to me and end up living on the streets." Or, "I'm going to do drugs and let them permanently damage my mind."

Of course not. We rarely intend to fall into sin, but too often it seems that we never intentionally intend *not* to fall into sin. In other words, we want to do right, but we're not vigilant.

I coached soccer for four years. In soccer, a goalie is sometimes called a keeper. The keeper's job is to prevent the opposing team from kicking the ball into the goal. He's constantly on the lookout, watching what's going on in the field. He's "keeping the net." Likewise, we need to keep our hearts, just as the goalie keeps the goal. Proverbs 4:23 instructs us, "Keep thy heart with all diligence; for out of it are the issues of life." When I think of the word *diligence* in this verse, a picture of consistent, disciplined vigilance comes into my mind. I think of a Christian actively seeking to ward off the "…sin which doth so easily beset us…" (Hebrews 12:1).

Satan is a major factor why we fall into sin. But he's not the only reason. James 1:14, the passage we looked at earlier, states, "But every man is tempted, when he is drawn away of his own lust, and enticed."

Be Vigilant about Our Own Weaknesses

All of us have weaknesses to which we're prone, and our own sinful flesh can tempt us to sin. For example, men often have weaknesses women don't, and vice-versa. There are personality weaknesses—an extrovert might struggle with sins toward which an introvert would be less inclined. Background can affect us—if we grew up in a Christian home, we'll struggle with some things that a child who grew up in a broken home would struggle with less, such as relying on our parents' relationship with the Lord instead of our own.

Generational sin is another personal weakness you might have. My father struggled greatly with anger, and I inherited that trait. Do I have a right to sin in anger because my father struggled with anger as well? No, of course not. But knowing that anger is something I'm prone to helps me to be vigilant.

Our past experiences aren't an excuse for our sin, but they may help us understand *why* we're struggling. They can help us pinpoint areas in our lives we need to fix or grow in. And this is why it is so important that we frequently evaluate ourselves. I'm not talking about casually deciding to work on something in your life when you get around to it. I'm talking about vigilance. We must consciously evaluate our weaknesses, and through the Holy Spirit's help, take action steps to grow stronger.

When we stop being vigilant in our Christian life, we stop growing. And when we stop growing, we become stagnant, lukewarm Christians who don't accomplish anything for the Lord. Vigilance is the first key in winning the battle over sin.

Victory Exercises for Vigilantly
Guarding Against Sin

As we conclude each chapter of this book, I want to give you practical exercises to put the truths of the chapter into action. These exercises are similar to the "homework" I give when I share the same truths in one-on-one counseling. If you picked up this book with a specific spiritual struggle for which you are seeking victory, I especially encourage you to answer each question and complete each assignment.

When are you most susceptible to your weakness? Is it at a certain time of the day? Or when you are with certain people? Do certain situations cause you to fall?

_____

_____

_____

_____

_____

_____

_____

_____

What specifically are your common areas of battle? Do you see them as a result of Satan's attacks or a personal weakness (such as something specific to your gender, personality, generational sins, etc.)?

_____

_____

_____

_____

_____

_____

_____

_____

_____

_____

_____

_____

_____

_____

Find an accountability partner. Is there someone
you trust, respect, and feel comfortable holding
you accountable? Consider a few guidelines as you
seek accountability:

- The person you are accountable to should be someone
  you could meet with every week for five to ten minutes.

- Write about three or four questions you want your
  partner to ask you every week about your battle area.

- Commit to being honest and transparent.

_____

_____

_____

_____

_____

_____

_____

_____

_____

_____

2

I - **Imagine** the Consequences

In September 2008, Diana Valencia was arrested on drug charges. She was clearly guilty (it's tough to explain two kilos of cocaine as an innocent mistake).

In a last-ditch effort, however, Valencia went to Judge Manuel Barraza for help. He told her that he might be able to prove her innocent…if she paid him a substantial sum of money. Valencia went to the FBI, and, along with her sister, concocted a plan to trap Barraza.

Ultimately, the FBI and Valencia's sister were able to record the judge agreeing to bribery. Consequently, Barraza was arrested and sentenced to prison time because of his dishonesty.[1]

I doubt Judge Barraza would have been so quick to agree to the bribe if he'd known the consequences. And I wonder if his story would have turned out differently had he taken a moment to stop and imagine the potential consequences of his actions.

There is always pleasure in sin for a season. I'm sure Judge Barraza already had a good idea of what he'd spend his newfound wealth on once he was paid. Sin *is* enjoyable, at least for a time. Hebrews 11:25 states, "Choosing rather to suffer affliction with the people of God, than to enjoy the pleasures of sin for a season." But eventually, our sin catches up to us. Maybe you've heard the old saying, "Sin always takes you further than you want to go. It always keeps you longer than you want to stay. And it always costs you more than you want to pay."

The truth is, we may not see the consequences for our sin today, next month, or even all of the consequences ten years from now. But one day, we will. Galatians 6:7–9 tell us, "Be not deceived; God is not mocked: for whatsoever a man

---

1. "Fifth Circuit Upholds Former Texas State Judge's Bribery-Related Convictions," *Prison Legal News*, December 15, 2012, https://www.prisonlegalnews.org/news/2012/dec/15/fifth-circuit-upholds-former-texas-state-judges-bribery-related-convictions/.

soweth, that shall he also reap. For he that soweth to his flesh shall of the flesh reap corruption; but he that soweth to the Spirit shall of the Spirit reap life everlasting. And let us not be weary in well doing: for in due season we shall reap, if we faint not."

Our actions always have consequences. When we begin to believe that we can live however we want without ever answering for our actions, the devil finds the perfect opportunity to gain a foothold in our lives.

So why such a big emphasis on consequences as we battle sin? Because sin, at least for a time, can bring us pleasure. And that pleasure can blind us to the pain down the road.

But we can only go so long without reaping the consequences of our actions. In fact, much of the book of Proverbs emphasizes this point. Repeatedly, we see an example of a sin and the consequences that follow it. Anger plus its consequences are listed six times. Drinking and its consequences are listed nine times. Bitterness and its consequences are listed three times. Solomon was carefully describing each of these consequences so specifically because he wanted his son to be aware of how serious and detrimental playing with sin is.

Every sin carries with it some form of pleasure. It's enjoyable not to forgive somebody. Essentially, we get to lock the person up in our fantasy and be the judge, the witness, and the prosecuting attorney. It's enjoyable to lie because it makes us look better to others than perhaps we really are. It's enjoyable to steal because we get something that we want. It's enjoyable to _____ (you fill in the blank). But the consequences will always outweigh the temporary enjoyment that we might get.

For example, there's pleasure in pornography—for a time. It satisfies your flesh, and it's something you can easily hide. And that's why it's crucial to think through the consequences. It is wise to think like this: "If I view pornography, my marriage could be destroyed. If I view pornography, I could rip my family apart and hurt my children for life. If I view pornography, I could lose the spiritual influence I have in the lives of those I teach or disciple. If I view pornography, I will become a slave to something that is highly addictive." What you gain by sinning is never worth what you lose by sinning.

If you're struggling with a specific sin, think about the consequences that could come from that sin. If you need to, write them down, using verses that describe consequences of the sin you're battling.

You might be struggling with alcohol. Proverbs 23:29–30 describes the consequences: "Who hath woe? who hath sorrow? who hath contentions? who hath babbling? who hath wounds without cause? who hath redness of eyes? They that tarry long at the wine; they that go to seek mixed wine." Although there is pleasure in drinking, at least for a time, drinking can ultimately rip families apart and cause wounds that should never have happened. It can cause people to commit actions they can't remember that will haunt them years later.

When we imagine the consequences of the sins we're dealing with, we're awakened to just how serious sin is. We recognize *why* it's so important to get victory over sin that we're struggling with. Too much is at stake with the consequences.

Victory Exercises for Imagining the
Consequences of Sin

Find Scripture examples and warnings of the
consequences of sin.

_____

_____

_____

_____

_____

_____

Write, memorize, and meditate on one passage that gives
consequences of the sin with which you are struggling.

_____

_____

_____

_____

_____

_____

Ask yourself, "Is the short pleasure of this sin worth the guilt and consequences the sin will bring?" Write the possible consequences of giving in to this sin.

_____

_____

_____

_____

_____

_____

List seeds/thoughts you planted in your mind yesterday. These could be good or bad. What kind of crop will those seeds produce tomorrow?

_____

_____

_____

_____

_____

3

C - **Cry** Out to God

Have you ever created a mess in your life that you knew was entirely your fault? For example, have you ever said something to your spouse that you immediately wished you could take back? After just one hastily-spoken sentence, you found yourself the recipient of the cold shoulder for several hours. Or have you maybe fired off an angry comment at someone on Facebook that, in retrospect, wasn't the wisest?

Perhaps you're dealing with more of a habitual sin. No matter how hard you try, you can't stop being negative. You can't stop gossiping. You can't take control of your thought life. You can't submit to authority. You can't read your Bible faithfully. You can't seem to attend church faithfully.

Oh, you've tried many times. In fact, you've even succeeded, at least for a few days or a week. But after about six or seven days, you're right back where you started. You're frustrated with yourself and wonder why you can't seem to get the victory over this habitual sin. At this point, you have two options. The devil whispers option one in your ear, saying, "This whole Christian life thing? You can't do it. Maybe *some* victory is possible, but definitely not *total* victory. Why even bother?"

But as believers, failure isn't our only choice, although the devil wants us to think that. The Lord gives us the other option: "But thanks be to God, which giveth us the victory through our Lord Jesus Christ" (1 Corinthians 15:57). This verse doesn't say, "But thanks be to God, which giveth us the victory over most things through our Lord Jesus Christ." It simply says that we have the victory.

Perhaps you're wondering, "That's great. But I've tried that—in fact, I've memorized that verse before. I believe it, but I don't know how to put it into action."

The secret is not in repeating words; it is in crying out to God for deliverance. You see, although we might be able to live victoriously, at least for a little while, we'll ultimately fail because we're accomplishing things in our own effort.

But when we cry out to God, He gives us His strength and enablement.

Remember that God delights in giving second chances—just look at the story of the Israelites throughout Judges. We see a repeated cycle throughout the book. The Israelites would fall into sin. Then, God would allow them to be taken captive as a consequence of their actions. In the middle of bondage, the Israelites would call out to God for a deliverer. God would listen, and the nation would enter a period of rest. But after just a short time, the Israelites would fall back into sin, beginning the cycle all over again.

Let's take a closer look: "And the children of Israel did evil in the sight of the LORD, and forgat the LORD their God, and served Baalim and the groves. Therefore the anger of the LORD was hot against Israel, and he sold them into the hand of Chushanrishathaim king of Mesopotamia: and the children of Israel served Chushanrishathaim eight years" (Judges 3:7–8).

The Israelites forgot God and began serving the false god Baal. As a result, the Lord grew angry and allowed them to be taken captive by the Mesopotamians. But the people cried out to God for a deliverer in verse 9, and the Lord heard them: "And when the children of Israel cried unto the LORD, the LORD raised up a deliverer to the children of Israel, who delivered them, even Othniel the son of Kenaz, Caleb's younger brother."

The same scenario repeats itself just a few verses later in verse 12. Israel, because of their sin, again entered bondage under the Moabites. Yet they cried out to God, and He delivered them into a period of rest. This is just one chapter in Judges—we can see the Israelites repeat this cycle consistently.

But what about us? Too often, it seems that we wake up in the morning, dedicated to following the Lord, but fall into the same sinful habit we've been trying to break for years before we even get to work. Maybe you've promised God that you're going to get up early to read your Bible and pray, but when your alarm goes off, you feel too tired and fall back to sleep. Or perhaps you've told the Lord you're going to be in church for every service that week, but you aren't...again. It might be that you promised the Lord you would work on not growing angry so easily. But you lose your temper the first day after you committed not to.

If you feel discouraged about the lack of progress you're making in the battle against sin, you and the Israelites have that in common. When the Israelites were confronted with the serious ramifications of their sin, they turned back to the Lord. They cried out to Him, begging Him for His forgiveness and deliverance. And nowhere do we see that the Lord refused to listen. He always answered and sent a deliverer.

It's the same for us. Every time we call out to God for deliverance from sin, He'll give us whatever we need to gain the victory. Never once will God say, "No, it's too late for you—you've asked for My help too many times. You're on your own."

That's not how our God operates. It's never too late for you to come to Him, asking for His forgiveness, strength, and enabling. The Bible doesn't say, "For a just man falleth one time, and sometimes riseth up again." It says, "For a just man falleth seven times, and riseth up again…" (Proverbs 24:16).

Cry out to God, tell Him you're struggling, and ask for His help for victory. I'm so thankful that "it is of the Lord's mercies that we are not consumed, because his compassions fail not. They are new every morning: great is thy faithfulness" (Lamentations 3:22–23). Every morning, God's mercies are new. We don't have to fear that God will turn us away when we cry out to Him for help with a sin we're struggling with.

At this point, you might be wondering, "Why is crying out to God so important? Why is this such a crucial step in gaining victory over our sin?"

First, it forces us to acknowledge that we have a problem in our lives, and it forces us to acknowledge the source of that problem. Sometimes we blame our circumstances, environment, or people around us for our sin. But when we genuinely cry out to God, we're saying, "Lord, I need You! I have a sin in my life that I can't conquer on my own!" It sounds pretty basic, but true change will never occur until we recognize that we have a problem we need to change. By crying out to God, we recognize that we have a sin problem only the Lord can remedy.

Second, it moves us to action. It takes us from the theoretical "I should probably work on this" to "God, I need You to help me work on this! I don't want this sin in my life anymore!" When we genuinely cry out to God, He'll give us wisdom to take active steps to conquer the sin we're struggling with.

Finally, crying out to God forces us to recognize the true source of victory over sin. The secret to victory isn't crying out to self or trying a little harder. The secret to true victory over sin is not trying *at all* in our own strength; it is crying out to God for His strength instead.

📝 Victory Exercises for Crying Out to God

Write, memorize, and quote Psalm 34:6 when
temptation comes.

_____

_____

_____

_____

_____

_____

Cry out to the Lord for deliverance, and let Him tell
you what to do as your step of faith. Keep a record of
His promptings.

_____

_____

_____

_____

_____

_____

Learn to cry out for forgiveness as soon as you have failed.
Write a prayer to God seeking forgiveness for your sin.

_____

_____

_____

_____

_____

_____

_____

_____

_____

_____

_____

4

T - **Take** Thoughts Captive

When you think about famous battles in history, several might come to mind. You might think of the Battle of Tours, when Charles Martel stopped the Muslim advance in Europe. Perhaps you'd think about the Battle of Antietam, the bloodiest single-day battle of the Civil War. You might recall the Battle of Waterloo, when Napoleon met his match once and for all. Perhaps you'd think of the Battle of the Bulge or D-Day during World War II.

Although those battles took place in different continents, were waged by different people for different causes, and had varying degrees of results, one thing is the same for all of them. All of them were physical battles fought on a physical battleground.

That's not so in the Christian's battle. Second Corinthians 10:3–4 tells us, "For though we walk in the flesh, we do not war after the flesh: (For the weapons of our warfare are not carnal, but mighty through God to the pulling down of strong holds;)." For the Christian, spiritual warfare takes place in the mind. And when we engage in the battle, the weapons that God gives us are powerful through Him. In fact, they are so powerful that they can pull down even the greatest stronghold in our lives. This is crucial—the Lord never intended for us to wage a battle in our flesh, but through His strength. And He's given us weapons—what I believe specifically are the Word of God and prayer—to accomplish that.

Whether we recognize it or not, the second we trusted Christ, we entered into spiritual battle. These battles come when we least expect it. They can come five minutes after we wake up in the morning or five minutes before we go to bed at night. They can come at church, in the carpool lane, as you drive your kids to school, on your way to an early-morning college class, at a high-pressure business meeting for work—at anytime and at any place.

Every Christian is going to struggle with a different spiritual battle, but we must recognize the one truth that remains the same. Each spiritual battle that we wage has a specific point of origin—our minds. Even when we're tempted to act on an outward sin, that temptation can be traced back to a thought. Paul, under the inspiration of the Holy Spirit, understood just how powerful thoughts are. He wrote in 2 Corinthians 10:5: "Casting down imaginations, and every high thing that exalteth itself against the knowledge of God, and bringing into captivity every thought to the obedience of Christ." That last half of our verse talks about taking into captivity every thought that we have.

Easier said than done though, right? How exactly do we take our thoughts captive? To answer that, let's start by looking at the first half of the verse. In our verse, we come to the phrase "casting down imaginations." *Imagination,* in this context, isn't referring to what you'd say to a five-year-old telling you about the purple-polka-dot monster that lives under his bed: "You have such an imagination!" In this verse, imagination means "conclusion," as in a mental summing up of thoughts or an assumption. (We find the same Greek word in Romans 3:28: "Therefore we *conclude* that a man is justified by faith without the deeds of the law.")

Making this distinction is hugely important because, in part, it helps us understand what *stronghold* means from the previous verse. A stronghold is any lie that we conclude (imagine) to be true. For example, a stronghold would be born out of consistently thinking, "I can't get victory over my anger, my lust, my moodiness—you fill in the blank." I've worked with young people for years, and I've had them tell me, "God can't use me. I've messed up too many times. I'm no good." That's a stronghold the devil has implanted in their minds because he wants to deceive them into thinking God can't use them.

Because we've let thoughts like those consistently replay in our minds, a stronghold has developed. We've *concluded* that we can't get victory. That imagination, however, is a lie from the devil. Through the Lord's enabling, we can get victory in our lives.

Second Corinthians 10:5 tells us that we are to bring into captivity every thought to the obedience of Christ. Our thought life is the essence of our spiritual battle. In fact, if we let our thoughts go, we have more often than not lost the battle. The Bible doesn't tell us to bring into captivity every desire, action, habit, or character trait. The Bible tells us to take every *thought* captive because our thoughts are the battleground. Thoughts turn into desires, and desires turn into actions. Then, those actions turn into habits, and while desires and actions are difficult to get victory over, habits are nearly impossible to defeat. But if we can take our thoughts captive, the devil is essentially defeated.

Almost twenty years ago, I heard a preacher share a practical way to take our thoughts captive that has been a help to me. He called it "the four-second rule," emphasizing that we are to *immediately* bring wrong thoughts into captivity. Although I couldn't give a specific Scripture reference that says four seconds is better than three or six seconds, I have found this rule helpful to following the biblical command of 2 Corinthians 10:5.

The four-second rule means we have four seconds to take a sinful thought captive. In about four seconds, lust conceives into sin. If we wait any longer, Satan has the perfect opportunity for a foothold. When a sinful thought jumps into your mind, attack it. Quote a verse. Cry out to the Lord. Ask Him for His enabling to get victory.

Ever since implementing this rule into my life, my spiritual walk has dramatically transformed. When we begin taking our thoughts captive quickly, our spiritual walk will transform.

Taking your thoughts captive quickly requires a game plan. Before the temptation comes, have a set plan of what to do to combat the temptation. First, I'd encourage you to pray—to cry out to God for deliverance. After that, replace the thought with something else: this may be verses you have prepared about the sin you're struggling with. It could be a 3x5 card you carry with you with a verse you are working to memorize; you could pull it out and redirect your thoughts to that passage. It may be that you sing a hymn, praise God for three specific things, or pray for a lost loved one, your pastor, or a struggling church member.

The next time temptation enters your mind, take the thought captive right away. This is essential. When we coddle sin, the devil immediately seizes on our hesitation. The key is to have a game plan. If you don't have a specific course of action you're ready to take when temptation comes, if you're not fully committed to immediately taking that thought captive, it's unlikely that you're going to win victory.

Victory Exercises for Taking
Thoughts Captive

Practice the four-second rule whenever a sinful thought
arises. Keep practicing this until it becomes a habit.

_____

_____

_____

Eliminate the sinful thought with a good thought
immediately (Philippians 4:8). Plan ahead a list of verses,
hymns, praises, or prayer requests to which you can turn
your mind. List your game plan here:

_____

_____

_____

Reckon yourself quickly that you are dead to the sin and
alive unto God (Romans 6:11–13). You don't have to keep
thinking about the sinful thought.

_____

_____

What are the false conclusions you may have made about the sin you're struggling with? Do any of these sound familiar?

- "I will never overcome this sin."

- "I deserve this sin."

- "This sin isn't that bad."

- "Everyone commits this sin."

Write out any that come to mind, and then write a verse to counter each—a truth you can use to cast down that false conclusion.

_____

_____

_____

_____

_____

_____

_____

_____

_____

5

O - **Observe** the Omnipresence of God

Have you ever had so much to do that you wish you could be in two or three places at once? If only you could drop the kids off at soccer practice, fold the four loads of laundry at home, and stop by the grocery store all at the same time, life would be smooth sailing.

Or if only you could catch an extra hour of sleep, go to the early morning classes, and finish all of your projects *at the same time*, school would be a breeze.

At some point in our lives, we've wished we could be in more than one place at once. But the Lord has never had this problem. Our God is *omnipresent*, meaning that He is present everywhere at all times. For me, this thought is both comforting and challenging.

It's comforting in that no matter where I go, Jesus is always with me. I think of the Psalm that states, "Whither shall I go from thy spirit? or whither shall I flee from thy presence? If I ascend up into heaven, thou art there: if I make my bed in hell, behold, thou art there. If I take the wings of the morning, and dwell in the uttermost parts of the sea; Even there shall thy hand lead me, and thy right hand shall hold me" (Psalm 139:7–10). We can't go anywhere where God is not already present. We can rest in the fact that we can never be too far from His care, protection, and love.

But just as this thought is comforting, it's also convicting. God sees everything I do, hears everything I say, and is aware of everything I think. Remembering the omnipresence of God is crucial in defeating temptation.

Years ago, Tom Farrell, a good friend of mine, told me that if there were one attribute of God to implant in the heart of a teenager to stay away from sin, it would be the omnipresence of God. He told me that it's difficult for a man to sin if he can sense the omnipresence of God at any moment.

Would it make a difference if your pastor went with you everywhere at every second? Of course it would. For some of us, I think our lives would completely change. What we sometimes fail to realize is that the Holy Spirit *is* constantly present with us. He sees everything—from our heart's motives to our outward actions. When we come face-to-face with this reality, our lives will change.

I think of seventeen-year-old Joseph in the Old Testament who was dropped into a completely corrupt, wicked culture. This wasn't his choice; he was forced into slavery by his brothers. He was dragged hundreds of miles from his home and placed into a strange household to serve as a slave to Potiphar, captain of the Egyptian guard. Because of his excellent testimony, however, the Lord allowed him to prosper in Potiphar's house. Slowly, things were starting to look up.

But everything changed for Joseph when Potiphar's wife began to pressure him to commit immorality with her. To an outsider looking in, this would seem to be the perfect opportunity for Joseph to retaliate against all the wrong that had been done to him. When we consider the high status of Potiphar (he was captain of the Egyptian guard), it's likely that his wife was beautiful. Joseph, a teenage boy who had been done a great wrong, could have easily justified, "It's okay for me to commit this sin. No one will know anyway—Potiphar is not even in the house."

Then one day, a defining moment in Joseph's life came. Potiphar's wife tempted him again, but this time she took action. Genesis 39:11-12 records the story: "And it came to pass about this time, that Joseph went into the house to do his business; and there was none of the men of the house there within. And she caught him by his garment, saying, Lie with me...."

Joseph, however, chose not to take the easy path. Instead of succumbing, the Bible says, "...and he left his garment in her hand, and fled, and got him out" (Genesis 39:12).

This leads me to ask: "Why did Joseph say no?"

Was he afraid of being caught by Potiphar?

Was he fearful of losing his position?

Was it a purity commitment he'd made at a Christian summer camp?

Was it his pastor's passionate preaching every Sunday morning?

Was it his parent's repeated admonitions against impurity?

To all of those questions, the answer is no. Joseph was completely alone in his fight against temptation. And by alone, I mean that he didn't even have the Bible, which had not yet been written. (Remember, this story is recorded in Genesis.) The reason behind his refusal is something even greater—something vital for each of us to grasp.

The reason Joseph had victory over temptation is because he recognized the omnipresence of God. He knew that God could see him in the house. The acute awareness of God's presence was the only thing he had.

Joseph said, "There is none greater in this house than I; neither hath he kept back any thing from me but thee, because thou art his wife: how then can I do this great wickedness, *and sin against God?*" (Genesis 39:9). Joseph was saying, "Ma'am, we're not alone here. God's watching us, even if no one else is around. I can't sin against God."

Joseph refused to commit immorality with Potiphar's wife because he knew God was watching him.

It's the same for us when we're confronted with temptation. Perhaps no one sees what's on your computer screen in the middle of the night, but God does. No one can read your thoughts, but God does. Your pastor doesn't see you when you yell at your kids and fight with your spouse, but God does. The Bible clearly tells us, "The eyes of the Lord are in every place, beholding the evil and the good" (Proverbs 15:3).

When we let this truth take hold of our minds, it will transform us. Our battle against sin won't be based on, "I hope I don't get caught." It will be based on, "God sees me. I can't do this."

When you're facing temptation, remember that God is watching. Let the knowledge of His presence change the way you live. One of the greatest keys in winning the battle over temptation is remembering and reflecting on God's omnipresence.

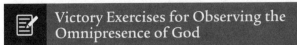

Imagine someone whom you greatly respect traveled with you wherever you went and was able to read your thoughts. How might that impact your struggle against sin? Then, substitute that person you respect with the Holy Spirit who is always with you.

_____

_____

_____

_____

_____

Write, memorize, and meditate on Proverbs 15:3.

_____

_____

_____

_____

_____

Acknowledge God's presence constantly by talking to Him.

_____

_____

_____

_____

Ask yourself, "Could I bring myself to give in to temptation when I know that God is constantly watching me?"

_____

_____

_____

_____

6

R - **Run** from Sin

When Jim and Trish Hughes boarded their yacht for a once-in-a-lifetime trip around the world, they had no idea that one Icelandic fisherman, Eriker Olafsson, would destroy their plans.

As the Hughes sailed on the British coast, Olafsson crashed into their yacht with his boat. Ultimately, the extensive repairs amounted to thousands of dollars. As a result, the Hughes were forced to abandon their trip to have their yacht fixed.

Undeterred, the Hughes attempted a second around-the-world-trip nearly a year later. Pausing for a break, they moored their yacht at Gosport, a town on the south coast of Hampshire. Meanwhile, Olafsson—the same fisherman who had derailed their plans last year—noticed the familiar yacht from a distance. Determined to apologize again for the accident, he sailed toward the yacht—and rammed into it by accident a second time.

Olafsson was arrested, and the Hughes lived in a motorboat until repairs could be made. When asked how they felt about the bizarre incident, Hughes responded, "What that man has done to me is absolutely incredible. I don't want him ever to apologize to me again. Both times he caused massive damage to the hull and mast. I can never rest sound or leave her alone again unless Olafsson has sailed off into the distance, never to return." He added, "I, for one, will never, ever sail anywhere near Iceland, just on the off-chance that he will be there."[1]

Jim Hughes was serious about avoiding another collision, even if it meant steering clear of Iceland. And that is the same attitude we need to have in avoiding temptation.

Throughout my life, I've heard pastors and Christians emphasize resisting temptation, and I wholeheartedly agree. The Bible tells us, "Submit yourselves therefore to God. Resist the devil, and he will flee from you" (James 4:7).

---

1   Stewart Payne, "Couple's round-the-world yacht dream twice scuppered by the drunken sailor," *The Telegraph*, August 23, 2003, https://www.telegraph.co.uk/news/uknews/1439598/Couples-round-the-world-yacht-dream-twice-scuppered-by-the-drunken-sailor.html.

It's true that temptation can come when we least expect it. How many times, for example, have you been minding your own business when a sinful thought from nowhere assaulted your mind? When those times come, we must immediately fight the temptation battling for our hearts. We must resist the devil.

But we shouldn't stop there. There is a big difference between resisting temptation and avoiding temptation, and if we *can* avoid temptation, we should. Understanding this is our sixth key to victory—running from sin.

If we avoid temptation—if we run from it—we don't have to resist it. In fact, God commands us, "Take fast hold of instruction; let her not go: keep her; for she is thy life. Enter not into the path of the wicked, and go not in the way of evil men. Avoid it, pass not by it, turn from it, and pass away" (Proverbs 4:13–15).

Did you catch all those commands about sin? Avoid sin. Pass not by sin. Turn from sin. Pass away from sin. Not, "Get as close as you can to sin without actually sinning." In our battle against sin, we must take active steps to not just resist sin, but to also avoid temptation to sin.

When you run from sin, you need to run to Scripture. Meditate on truth. Grab hold of a verse that speaks specifically of the sin you're struggling with, and let it sink into your heart. Run to the Lord, and ask Him to give you wisdom, direction, and strength to get victory over the sin that you're struggling with.

Daily, we need to ask the Lord to deliver us from evil. In Matthew 6:13 Jesus taught us to pray, "And lead us not into temptation, but deliver us from evil: For thine is the kingdom, and the power, and the glory, for ever. Amen."

You will never have victory in the Christian life until you learn how to run fast and far from sin.

So, what does this "running" look like on a practical level? For one, it means getting rid of items or objects (physical or digital) that could cause you to be tempted. For example, if you struggle with listening to the wrong kinds of music, memorize verses to help you—that's foundational. But don't stop there—delete songs on your phone, toss your CDs, even tear the radio out of your car if you need to. This might seem extreme, but running from sin is something we need to be extreme about.

Remember Joseph from our last chapter? He didn't just stick around after Potiphar's wife tempted him; he ran out so quickly he left his coat in the hands of Potiphar's wife. He recognized that sin wasn't to be trifled with, and he fled.

My two sons and I have a program on our computers called Covenant Eyes. It accounts for all of the websites that we've visited and compiles a report all three of us can see. This is one way that my family runs from sin. By having these precautionary measures, we keep each other accountable. I'm trying to not just resist temptation, but also have accountability in place to avoid temptation.

Another way we run from sin is to avoid people or situations that draw us into sin. This is what Proverbs 4:14–15 directly warns against: "Enter not into the path of the wicked, and go not in the way of evil men. Avoid it, pass not by it, turn from it, and pass away."

If there are friends who have a way of pulling you into sins over which you're trying to get victory, don't spend extended time with them. If there are places where you know you'll be more likely to be tempted or your resistance to temptation will be lower, don't go.

Before temptation comes, run from it! Like Joseph, don't spend time thinking or contemplating sin. The more you think about it, the more likely you are to succumb to it. Don't let temptation take up space in your mind—flee from it.

Victory Exercises for Running from Sin

Recall the places where you tend to be tempted. It could
be walking past the magazine section of the grocery shop
or driving past a certain billboard. Decide to deliberately
avoid these places. List alternative routes you can
take instead.

_____

_____

_____

_____

_____

Run from the thought of temptation in your mind to the
Scriptures. Start by memorizing 1 Corinthians 10:13. Try
quoting it in twelve seconds. By the time you are done
quoting it, you will have forgotten the temptation.

_____

_____

_____

_____

Decide not only to resist sin but also to avoid it by not getting close (Proverbs 4:15).

_____

_____

_____

_____

_____

In the days ahead, keep a record of the times you were tempted with sin and how you ran from it.

_____

_____

_____

_____

_____

_____

_____

_____

_____

Study Joseph's response to temptation in Genesis 39:7–12. What do you see in his story that you can apply to your battle with temptation?

_____

_____

_____

_____

_____

_____

_____

_____

_____

7

Y - **Yield** to the Spirit

We've covered a lot of ground. We've talked about the importance of vigilance in our battle against temptation. We've discussed the importance of imagining the consequences of our actions and taking our thoughts captive. We've talked about crying out to God and remembering His omnipresence. We've even mentioned the importance of running from sin to avoid temptation, not just resisting it.

But I have one final word of encouragement for you: I know that you cannot do it!

Yes, you read that right—you *can't* do it. You can't win the battle against sin. The devil is too powerful. All of the points we just discussed are too difficult for you and for me to do alone.

So what do we do? Do we put down this book, throw our hands up in despair, and admit defeat?

Absolutely not.

This final key to victory that we're going to discuss is crucial to winning the Christian battle.

We must yield to the Spirit. I believe that the greatest verse on sanctification in the Bible is Romans 8:13, which states, "For if ye live after the flesh, ye shall die: but if ye through the Spirit do mortify the deeds of the body, ye shall live."

When we live after the flesh—that is, when we try to accomplish anything, even good things, in our strength—we're going to fail. But if we, through the Holy Spirit, live for the Lord, we'll win the victory.

Years ago, I attended a pastor's conference and heard a man speak. He told a story about his six-year-old son, and it never left me. One Saturday, the pastor was out doing yardwork with his son. He brought out an edger to trim the grass growing up to the sidewalk, and his son excitedly asked, "Daddy, can I help you?"

He responded, "No, son, it's dangerous. Look at the sparks. You need to get back."

A little discouraged, the son sat on the front porch. Finally, his father finished with the edger and brought out a weed-eater. Again, the boy begged, "Daddy, can I help you?" And again, this pastor told his son no—a weed-eater was too dangerous.

Once the pastor finished with the weed-eater, he brought out a lawn mower. The same exchange happened between the father and the son. Finally, the pastor thought of something his son could do. He brought out a blower from the garage and handed it to his son. "You can blow off the driveway," he said.

Leaving his son to the task, he walked back into the garage to clean his tools. Several minutes passed, but he still didn't hear the blower. He walked outside to see his son on all fours blowing with his mouth.

"Son, what are you doing?" he questioned. His son responded, "You told me to blow off the driveway!"

Laughing, the pastor pointed to the blower. "Use this! It will be a lot easier."

I doubt any of us would blow off a driveway with our mouths, but in our spiritual lives, we can essentially do the same thing. We try to accomplish something in our own power without the Lord. It's as futile as trying to blow off a driveway with our mouths instead of using the blower.

God never intended for us to live the Christian life in our strength. He wants to give us His strength so that we can live the Christian life through Him. You see, if we try to live for the Lord by ourselves, we might succeed for a few days, weeks, or even months. But after a while, we'll fail. What gives us victory in the Christian life has nothing to do with our discipline or will power. What gives us victory in the Christian life is yielding to the spirit of God.

By now, you might be wondering, "Okay, so how does all of this work together? How do I take the steps that we've talked about and implement them, all the while yielding to the Spirit?"

It's crucial that we grasp the answer to this question. In fact, success in our Christian life in part hinges on understanding what it means to yield to the Spirit. When temptation comes tomorrow—and it will—how do you yield to the Spirit?

First, you have to get real about the sin in your life. You have to realize that the sin you're struggling with is a big deal to God. If there's a sin you're battling with in your life, I'd encourage you to take a few moments to talk to the Lord about it. Tell the Lord that you are struggling. Admit to Him that you're not quite sure how to get victory, but that you want to. As we've mentioned before, God never turns someone away who comes to Him in earnest, asking for His help. Commit to the Lord that, with His help, you want to get victory over this sin.

You see, getting victory over sin requires taking a step of faith. It requires telling the Lord that, while you're not sure of the next step to take, you know that He will show you and that you're committed to following it when He does.

After you take that step of faith, it's time to get busy. When temptation comes, stop. Tell the Lord, "God, here's the temptation—will You take that from me right now? Will You show me what step to take?"

When we're willing to yield to the Spirit, asking Him for help, He will help us. For example, you might be struggling with what you watch on television. When the temptation comes and you yield to the Spirit, He might prompt you to turn the TV off, quote a verse, and pray for a lost loved one.

You might be struggling with your thought life. When you yield to the Spirit, asking Him for strength and help, He might prompt you to quote a verse and sing a hymn.

As Christians, the Holy Spirit gives us the power to get victory over sin. But this requires a willingness to first submit to Him. God did not save us to live a defeated life. God saved us to live victoriously.

Victory Exercises for Yielding to the Spirit

List the weapons you can give the Holy Spirit to use when you decide to yield to Him. These could be:

- A song or two you can sing

- Specific verses you can quote

- Prayer requests for which you are burdened

- Imagining the consequences of yielding to the sin

_____

_____

_____

_____

Over the next few days, keep a record of the times you specifically yielded to the Holy Spirit and the step of faith He gave you in response.

_____

_____

_____

_____

Practice yielding to the Spirit in four seconds.

_____

_____

_____

_____

Memorize this formula for victory:

- Be on guard that you could fall at any moment.

- Ask God for help because He is with you.

- Follow the step He prompts you to take within four seconds.

- Experience in Christ the joy of victory over the temptation!

- Get ready for the next temptation (Proverbs 4:23).

_____

_____

_____

_____

_____

_____

CONCLUSION

Victory Is for You

When I think of great Christians in the Bible, I think of the apostle Paul. If there's one person we'd think had his Christian life together, it would be our friend Paul.

But in Romans 7, Paul was incredibly open about his struggles: "For the good that I would I do not: but the evil which I would not, that I do. Now if I do that I would not, it is no more I that do it, but sin that dwelleth in me. I find then a law, that, when I would do good, evil is present with me" (Romans 7:19–21). I picture Paul standing here, conflict on his face, as he writes to the Christians of his struggle.

He continues, "For I delight in the law of God after the inward man: But I see another law in my members, warring against the law of my mind, and bringing me into captivity to the law of sin which is in my members."

In effect, "I want to do right...but I don't want to do right either. There's such a conflict in my heart!"

Finally, he summarizes, "O wretched man that I am! who shall deliver me from the body of this death?"

Can you relate to that conflict? I know I can. But I'm so thankful that Paul didn't stop there. He continued, answering his own question, "I thank God through Jesus Christ our Lord. So then with the mind I myself serve the law of God; but with the flesh the law of sin."

That's the secret to victory: Jesus Christ our Lord. He already conquered sin and death and earnestly desires to give us victory in the Christian life.

Vigilantly guard against sin. Be on guard for sin that can creep its way into your heart and mind.

Imagine the consequences. Sin's effects are never worth it. Sin always causes more devastation than the temporary pleasure we receive from it.

Cry out to God. Ask Him for the victory that He promises and the direction to defeat your temptation.

Take thoughts captive. Immediately take every sinful thought captive, and replace it with truth from God's Word.

Observe the omnipresence of God. He sees the hidden sins that no one else does, and He's always present in our lives.

Run from sin. Don't just resist temptation, take steps to avoid it all together.

Yield to the Spirit. You can't accomplish the above steps in your own strength. It's too difficult, and you'll fail—every time. You have to ultimately rely on the Lord to give you strength.

God doesn't just want your pastor, Sunday school teacher, or spiritual mentor to live the victorious Christian life—He wants *you* to live the victorious Christian life. No matter if you've been saved for three weeks, three years, or thirty years, you can get victory. In the Lord's strength, you can experience victory in the battle against sin and temptation.

BOOKS WE THINK YOU WILL LOVE...

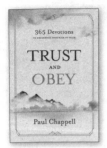

Trust and Obey
365 Devotions to Encourage Your Walk of Faith

Paul Chappell's Trust and Obey devotional will encourage your spiritual growth. The readings conclude with a solid takeaway principle which you can apply to your life immediately. You'll be challenged and encouraged to follow Jesus more closely and to walk with Him in practical ways throughout each day.

Are We There Yet?
Marriage—The Perfect Journey for Imperfect Couples

This book is for every couple at any stage of the marriage journey. It will help reveal a God-given perspective that can change and strengthen your marriage. A companion guide is sold separately.

Making Home Work in a Broken Society
Bible Principles for Raising Children and Building Families

God has entrusted you, as a parent, to care for and raise your children for Him—but it's not easy. Discover what it means to invest in your children and how you can bring them up in the nurture and admonition of the Lord.

STRIVINGTOGETHER.COM

ALSO AVAILABLE AS EBOOKS